He Waited for Me

He Waited for Me

PATRICIA A. KAMRADT

iUniverse, Inc.
New York   Bloomington

He Waited for Me

iUniverse books may be ordered through booksellers or by contacting:

iUniverse
1663 Liberty Drive
Bloomington, IN 47403
www.iuniverse.com
1-800-Authors (1-800-288-4677)

Because of the dynamic nature of the Internet, any Web addresses or links contained in this book may have changed since publication and may no longer be valid. The views expressed in this work are solely those of the author and do not necessarily reflect the views of the publisher, and the publisher hereby disclaims any responsibility for them.

ISBN: 978-1-4502-5304-8 (sc)
ISBN: 978-1-4502-5306-2 (dj)
ISBN: 978-1-4502-5305-5 (ebk)

Printed in the United States of America

iUniverse rev. date: 09/02/2010

In Memory of My Father

Contents

ACKNOWLEDGMENTS

Thanks to God for answering my prayers.

My adoptive parents, Margaretrose and Clifford, for taking me into their hearts.

My husband Bob and children, Robin, Joseph, and Chrystal, for their love.

My grandchildren, Eryka, Alyssia, Joshuel, and Nayelis, for being the lights of my life.

My brother James for his love and support throughout my life.

Introduction

So many years have come and passed;
God has chosen to unite us at last.
Treasure time we have together now;
Never take for granted the gift he has given, or ever doubt his
infinite wisdom.
My past will always remain in my heart, but a new door has
opened for us as father and daughter with a new beginning, a
brand new start.
Love,
Pat

I read my poem to my biological father, standing within an arm's reach of him, in his home in Delaware. My father would pass away a month later, after my meeting him for the first time. Alanis Morissette's song "Ironic" kept playing in my head: "And isn't it ironic … don't you think?" There must have been some divine intervention at play; after all, he did wait for me. I was close to fifty years old and had started my search for him only eight months prior to our meeting.

I hope this book will help my family understand the impact that meeting my biological father had on my life. People who are not adopted may not fully comprehend the intrinsic need to know one's history and heritage. You can love and be loved deeply by your adoptive parents and still feel this need.

Pieces of the puzzle were missing in my life, as they are with many other adoptees out there. I hope this will give some of them the courage to search and get answers, as I have. My search has been a long journey from start to finish, but well worth it.

I know this has been a life-changing experience for me. I hope it will be as positive an outcome for others who decide to search. There are no guarantees in life, but sometimes we need to take that leap of faith.

Chapter 1

Bringing Baby Home

As a young child, I was told I had been adopted through Catholic Charities, located in Chicago, Illinois. I learned from my adoptive parents that my given birth name had been Catherine, and that I had been named after my grandmother and great-grandmother, who were born in Ireland. Catholic Charities, I would come to find out later, tried to match adoptees with adoptive parents of similar heritage and religion. My adoptive mother's name was Margaretrose and my father's name was Clifford. They were both from the Chicago area and in their early

3

forties at the time of my adoption. They had desperately wanted to have children of their own but for medical reasons could not. The process of adoption was a long and difficult journey for them, but they brought home their first child, my brother James, in 1955, and I would soon follow, three years later in 1958.

Both Jim and I were only a few weeks old when we were adopted. Even though we were not biological siblings, we have always been close and consider ourselves to be brother and sister still to this day. We share a very close bond. My parents always told us that because we were adopted, we were special—we were chosen.

I didn't give being adopted much thought in my younger years; it just seemed normal. I was too busy being a kid. I can't remember my friends ever questioning it either. I guess they just accepted it too.

We were raised in a small Midwestern town in a suburb of Chicago. It was a friendly town where everyone knew each other's names. Not exactly Mayberry but close to it. It was a family-oriented, mostly middle-class town, and we enjoyed a simple kind of life there. Jim and I were typical siblings, fighting like cats and dogs at times but loyal to one another, sticking up for each other whenever it was needed. When we were younger, we had the same childhood

As I mentioned, Catholic Charities tried to match up adoptees with families of a similar heritage. I had been no exception. My mother Margaretrose's family was from County Clare, Ireland. Her brother Jack had his own spot on a local radio station called *The Irish Hour*. Every Sunday, without fail, we had the radio tuned in to hear him talk about Ireland and play Irish music. The first time I heard the Celtic music I was hooked; my mother told me it must be in my blood. Because of my love, I was enrolled in an Irish step dancing school taught by my uncle Joe. I can remember my father driving to Chicago every week to take me to classes. The building was an old empty factory building on Michigan Avenue, converted into a large dance studio. I was about eight or nine years old and can remember how proud I was that my uncle Joe was teaching me Irish dancing. He had about fifty or more students, all at different levels and age groups. We all wore black tap shoes. I can remember the sound they made on the wooden floors when we would all dance together. It sounded just like thunder and made the hairs on my arms stand up. I am certain I still remember how to do the Irish Jig and Reel but have not attempted either dance in a very long time.

My adoptive father, Clifford, was of German descent and worked as a city bus mechanic for the CTA in Chicago. He was on the short side, about five foot four, and had an olive complexion, brown eyes, and wore dark-rimmed glasses. As far back as I can remember he wore his hair in a crew cut, probably stemming back from his Air Force days when he served as a mechanic fixing the planes. During my childhood, he would leave for work at five every morning heading to Chicago's bus garages and would return at five every night, taking the train there and back. He had the distinct smell of motor oil on his uniform when he walked in the door; every day he was exhausted, as it was a hard job.

My mother always had dinner ready as soon as my dad walked in the door. We always sat down as a family for dinner and said grace before we ate. We would talk about our day, and my brother and I had to ask to be excused from the table before we could leave. My mother was a stay-at-home mother, but she did a lot of ironing for our church, such as pressing the altar boy garments, right in our kitchen; there were always stacks of clothes piled up in various places. She would move her ironing board from place to place where needed.

In her younger years, I heard my mother was stunning, with jet black hair and blue eyes. Because of health issues, as she got older she put on a lot of weight. She stood about five foot three and had a beautiful round face. She had a noticeable scar that ran from the top of her hairline all the way down to her brow line, directly in the center of her forehead. This scar was the result of a terrible car accident. Her aunt had been driving, and the story was told that a cab had cut my aunt off, and she sped after him. A horrific accident occurred, and my mother was ejected from the car and ended up coming to rest on the cement curb, head first. Her pituitary gland was damaged, which ended up affecting her health throughout her life. This, I came to find out later, may have contributed to her not being able to have children. When I was younger I didn't give it much thought, but throughout my life my mother rarely would leave the house, in fact, I could count on one hand the times that she had. I wonder if this too could have been a result of the accident.

On a few occasions, we went to her brother Jack's house, which was only a short distance from our house. She always got dressed up in her best Sunday clothes when she visited him, and I can remember the smell of the Channel No. 5 cologne that she wore. Even today, that smell reminds me of her. I know she thought the world of her brother Jack and always said how very proud she was of him. I remember only one family vacation where

A lot of my time during those years was spent away from my house going to the neighborhood community swimming pool. It was my saving grace. During summer break I taught myself how to swim and dive off the board. I was an independent child and entered many swimming competitions and even won a few ribbons. I can remember my father showing up at the pool to watch me in one of the competitions—it meant a lot to me that he did.

Another passion growing up was music. I believe I grew up in the best generation for music; no other era in my opinion can even come close, although I'm sure every generation would argue with me and say theirs was the best. I just couldn't get enough of it from Motown to rock 'n' roll, from the Beatles to the Rolling Stones, and all points in between. I remember when I was nine years old, my dad set up a turntable and some old speakers in our basement. The first album I played was *Magical Mystery Tour* by the Beatles. I had never heard anything like it before and was thrilled by it! I was hooked; there was no turning back, Both American and British songwriters were at the top of their games, competing with each other to our benefit. I had a strong connection with music during that time. I would immerse myself into it, and the super groups would keep on coming—one better than the next. I could go into my room, shut the door, put on an album, and shut the rest of the world out, just like millions of other kids did too, I'm sure.

That amazing music couldn't have come at a better time with the Vietnam War going on. So many young men being cut down at their prime of life, so many senselessly slaughtered. America needed something to divert people's attention, if only for a little while, to help us all cope with the grim reality of everything going on during this era. The Vietnam War and the Kennedy's being shot and Martin Luther King's assassination—it was all too much to deal with.

Lighthearted TV shows also came into play during this time with comedies like *I Love Lucy* and *The Dick Van Dyke Show*. This was just what people needed, and became what society wanted to portray as the perfect nuclear family. The father was always the breadwinner and chief disciplinarian, while the mother was the perfect stay-at-home nurturer. Without the music and comedy shows to help us through this most difficult time, it would have certainly been a lot harder to cope. I believe it was a godsend.

Looking back, I'm sure my father must have had a hard time dealing with my mother's illnesses. She suffered from diabetes, seizures, thyroid issues, and more than likely some form of depression. He was basically trying to raise my brother and me by himself. Most of the time he was very strict and it was his way or nothing. He was always very critical of us. At the time, I didn't understand why he was so harsh, but looking back I can see that he was dealing with his own heartaches. He did the best he could raising us. After all, he had grown up during the Depression era, and I'm sure things were hard on him too when he was young.

The hardest times for my brother and me were when we were in high school, and my mother would rarely come out of her bed. She would literally beg me to stay home with her from high school. I did do it often, but after awhile my attendance really suffered, and I couldn't take more time off from school. On many occasions I had to turn her down, and she would cry as I left for school. I remember feeling extremely guilty for not staying home with her, but could not do it anymore.

I did have enough sense during this time to realize that I needed to graduate from school. I don't want to portray myself as a saint by any means; I had a few friends I hung out with and would get in trouble just like most other rebellious teens.

When I was a senior in high school, one tragic event stands out in my mind. My mother was a chain smoker, and one night she fell asleep while smoking. Her nightgown caught on fire and burned her severely. I had just fallen asleep in my room, and my father was in the basement doing laundry. I woke up that night to my father screaming my mother's name, "Oh my God, Peg, what have you done!" He had carried her into the bathroom and was soaking her with water. I remember trying to enter the bathroom to help him and be with my mother, but he told me not to come in—he didn't want me to see her. I will never forget his voice. He was in tears and told me to call an ambulance. I remember thinking it was so odd that considering the extent of her burns, she wasn't screaming in pain; maybe she was in shock, I don't know for sure.

She was taken to Loyola Hospital in Melrose Park, which had the best burn unit in the country at the time. Her recovery there was slow as she was burned over a third of her body. The burns covered her left chest and entire side. They needed to do several skin grafts, taking skin from her thighs to cover the burned area. I remember the doctors saying that there was also a risk of infection occurring. The first time I entered her hospital room, I broke down in tears seeing her blackened skin and the extent of her burns. I can't even imagine the pain she was going through. I will never forget on my first visit, when she turned to me and pleaded with me to give her a cigarette. I thought, "How crazy is that?" Because of this incident, my father needed to refinance the house to pay for what the insurance wouldn't cover.

Although there were many sad memories, there were also many great ones too. The best memories I have of my adoptive mother were earlier, when she was able to leave her room and watch old movies in the living room with us. The ones that really stood out in my mind were *Little Women*, *I Remember Mama*, *It's a Wonderful Life* with Jimmy Stewart, and Shirley Temple movies like *Heidi*. My mother and I connected when we watched movies together. We would laugh and cry together. I do have fond memories of her laughter—it was lighthearted and boisterous and would fill up the room. She used to talk on the phone to her best friend Peggy for hours at a time, laughing. I loved my mom to the fullest and she loved me. She gave of herself as much as she could under the circumstances with her health issues. I grieved when she passed away when she was sixty-three from a stroke. I had just turned twenty-two years old, and Jim was twenty-five.

Following my mother's death, my father moved to a small town in Wisconsin, and he met a lady friend there. I was happy that he had someone he could talk to after losing my mother so young in life. My brother and I visited him quite often. We got along with him better now that we were older and had moved away from home. He lived about ten years after my mother's passing, and I think he had some happy times in Wisconsin. He was a good man who did the best he could with us; we both know he tried.

With my father's passing, both of my adoptive parents were gone. I found myself thinking more and more about my history and heritage. I once read that an adopted child's life is like a big puzzle with pieces missing. Until you find the missing pieces, you will never be truly whole. Doing a search for my biological parents had never previously even entered my thoughts. Now that I was older, such thoughts seemed to come often, consuming me at times. Now I wanted some answers, I needed to know. Yet these thoughts would be put on the back burner for a while longer as I married Bob, one of my brother Jim's best friends.

I fell in love with Bob the first time I saw him. I still remember the blue zip-up jacket he wore when he came to my house to see if

Jim was home. I also remember asking Jim who "that guy" was, as I thought he was really cute. Next thing you know, we went to a Jeff Beck concert together, and it was as if we had known each other for years. We got married within a year and a half. I was turning twenty and Bob twenty-one. We were married in a Catholic church; it was not a large wedding by any means, but our families and our friends were there and that was all we needed. Because of my adoptive mother's health issues, she couldn't make it to my wedding, which this broke my heart. After the ceremony, we went to my home to visit my mother before the reception. I think it meant a lot to her that we did, and I know it meant a lot to me. Bob and I went on to have three children, all within two years of each other; their names are Robin, Joseph, and Chrystal. The years that followed provided me a full-time job raising the kids. We struggled with life and money problems just like any other young family trying to make it.

Although my children brought much love and joy into my life, I still felt a void. No matter how much I tried to dismiss the feeling, I could not. I felt the need to find out basic information about my background, my history. This longing to find one's beginning, to know whose blood flows through your veins, is an intrinsic need. I knew that one day my children would be curious just like I was—after all, this was their history too. Because of this and because of the void I felt, I was compelled to try to get some of these basic questions, at very least my health background and my heritage, answered.

Chapter 2

Bits and Pieces

Most adoptees search for their biological mothers because of the maternal bond. I was no exception. Sixteen years after my adoptive mother Margaretrose passed away, I actively began my search for answers. I was thirty-eight years old, and by this time my children were grown. I felt I finally had time in my life to dedicate to this process of searching. I was thrilled by the prospect of finding answers that I felt I not only needed but also deserved.

All I really knew from my past was that my given name had been Catherine, the date of my birth, and the name of the agency that I was adopted from so long ago. I also knew I was born at Lewis Memorial Hospital, once located on Chicago's Michigan Avenue, but now closed. I knew this because I saw my birth certificate, and it had the name of the hospital on it—amended, of course, to have my adoptive parents' names added. Because this was all I knew, I felt I was going into my search blindly. I didn't really know how to go about it, where to begin, or how to start.

I remember asking God for his help doing this; he has always answered my prayers before. I told myself to keep the faith. I decided to write a simple letter to the family courts in the county where I lived, asking for help to do my search and advice on where I should begin. I actually received a letter back from a kindly judge saying he had looked up my adoption files. He told me I was adopted through Catholic Charities, which confirmed what my adoptive parents had told me, and added that I needed to inquire at Cook County where my adoption was finalized. He said that I could request nonidentifying information from Catholic Charities, and that was where I should begin my search. I was grateful that he actually took the time to write me back; he truly was instrumental in helping me get started. The next day I called Catholic Charities and told them I was interested in finding out anything I could.

At that time, birth records were sealed and closely guarded, but what that judge had told me was right; I at least had access to nonidentifying information. The caseworker I spoke with at the adoption agency said she would send me paperwork that I needed to fill out, have notarized, and send back. I thanked her and told her I would take what I could get.

After filling out and returning the basic paperwork as instructed, my letter with the nonidentifying information arrived.

The letter read:

Dear Patricia,

We have received your request for background information, and I am happy to be able to help you. We fully understand and appreciate an adopted person's very natural need to know something about his/ her biological heritage and the circumstances of the adoption. The Illinois adoption law requires mutual consent, which means we must have the written permission of both the adoptee and the birth parent before identifying information of any kind can be legally shared. We do not have permission from your birth mother. We shall place your name on our permanent registry of persons seeking information, and should your birth mother ever inquire in the future, we would inform her of your interest and you of her inquiry. For now, we are happy to share the following:

Your birth mother, whom we shall call Mary, approached our agency for assistance in January of 1958. She was referred by her parish priest and was accompanied to the initial interview by her mother. Mary requested housing, medical care, and adoption planning for her expected child. Mary entered one of our mutual services homes where child care and light housekeeping are exchanged for room and board and a small stipend. Mary made a good adjustment here and remained until delivery. Mary was a single Catholic girl of Swedish and Irish descent. She was a high school graduate and was employed doing office work. She impressed us a nice young girl, cooperative in counseling, and most anxious to make the best plan for you.

The record reads:

"She's a very attractive and well-groomed girl and was composed throughout the interview." Mary was from a stable, middle-class family. Mary had two younger siblings unaware of the pregnancy, but Mary's parents were involved and supportive. They agreed with

Mary's plan of adoption as being best for all concerned, especially for you. Mary named her steady boyfriend as your birthfather. He was a nineteen-year-old single protestant man of French and English descent. He was a senior in high school and worked part time. There is no further file on your birth father, and there is nothing at all on his extended family. Your birth parents dated for a while and considered marriage. Personal differences arose between them, however, and their relationship ended. Your birth father admitted paternity but was not involved in the planning for you.

Under the circumstances, Mary felt that adoptive placement would be the best for all concerned, especially for you. Single parenting was not readily accepted in those days, and Mary had traditional family values. She wanted you to have a stable two-parent home with a normal family life. She wanted you to have the advantages that she was unable to offer at that time. The decision to relinquish one's child is never easy, of course, but we have learned from experience that adoption is often the mature choice of a caring and realistic parent, made in the best interest of her child.

You were born, as you know, on June 19, 1958 at Lewis Memorial Hospital (now closed) in Chicago. Pregnancy and delivery were without complication, and you were born a normal, full-term

infant weighing 6 pounds 9 1/4 ounces. On June 24, 1958, Mary
signed the adoption surrender. You were baptized in St. Vincent's
Chapel and the sacrament was subsequently registered in Holy Name
Cathedral Parish. On August 4, 1958, you were placed with your
family. You had been eagerly anticipated and were joyfully received.
We hope this brief history has answered some of your questions on the
circumstances of your adoption.

You can be sure there was much love and careful planning that
went into your placement, from your birth mother and your adoptive
parents, as well as from our agency.

I was so excited when I read the letter. This was the first
tangible thing that I would hold and read about my biological
parents. Others probably take knowing about their birth
for granted. I did not. I felt I had at least a glimpse into my
beginnings. I read the letter to my children and told them this
was their history too.

I remember reading it time and time again and interpreting it
differently depending upon what mood I was in at the time. The
part that bothered me was that my mother had been from a stable,
middle-class family. The adoption took place not because of her

and her family's economic status, but because of the illegitimate status of her child—me.

That letter pacified me for about seven years, but when I was turning forty-four years old, I wanted more answers.

I never had regrets about being adopted, only questions surrounding it. I feel and have always felt that I have the God-given right to know these answers. I loved my adoptive parents, although at times I did feel disconnected from them. I feel adoptees can have a picture-perfect upbringing and still have the very basic need to know their history. It's a natural desire and should not be looked at negatively but as a positive, healthy desire.

Unlike me, my brother Jim never wanted to do a search for his biological parents. I never wanted to press the issue with him, as he seemed to feel that they had given him up, more or less abandoned him, and he wanted nothing more to do with it. It may be that a lot of males feel this way about searching for their birth parents; it would be interesting to do a study on this topic. My brother feels content about not knowing, where I am the opposite. In my opinion, finding this out is the foundation on which all is built. It is not the whole picture, but it is definitely a piece needed to complete the puzzle.

Chapter 3

Confidential Intermediary

As I became older, my curiosity never diminished; it only grew. The thought crossed my mind that maybe I was too late. What if they were both already dead? It could be possible. If I was going to do a search for them, I had better do it now. I kept telling myself that I only wanted basic background information, maybe as a way to protect myself from hurt or disappointment. As I felt that I had exhausted my search with Catholic Charities, it was time to move on.

I ended up looking on the Internet and found an agency sponsored by the state of Illinois. It sounded reliable. The program was called a *confidential intermediary service*, which would help adoptees to search for their biological parents. I called the agency and asked for a packet on what was involved and how I could get started. I received the packet in the mail soon afterward and read it from front to back. I started to feel optimistic about searching.

Even though I was older, I still had that longing inside to find out more.

By now, there was no denying that finding out more information was consuming my life. I knew that I couldn't rest until I had some answers. Since time could be running out, I now felt as if I was on a mission.

I think all adoptees have the right to find out answers. We are not an island unto ourselves; we all came from somewhere. And I had children and grandchildren who one day could want answers too, so I told myself I was not only doing the search for myself but also for them.

The brochure I received in the mail stated if you were an adult adoptee, a birth parent of an adult adopted person, or an adopted parent of a minor and the adoption was legally completed in Illinois, filing a petition for the appointment of an intermediary might be a good choice. Because it is a court-ordered search, the confidential intermediary has access to information from court files and agency records. For that reason, the potential for locating the person you are seeking is often greater than other search options may offer. I needed to petition the court in Cook County because that was where my adoption was finalized. Within the brochure the service sent me was the actual petition, which I could fill out on my own or have a lawyer complete. I knew a lawyer would probably charge me quite a large fee for this service, and I thought it looked pretty simple; so I filled it out, crossed my fingers, had it notarized, and sent it in.

Within a couple of weeks I received a court date in the mail stating the judge would hear my case. It stated I could be there in person or not. I remembered being excited that the petition worked and that the judge would actually listen to my case. It would take a few months, but waiting was something I was good at by now.

I finally received the letter in the mail I waiting for—the outcome from my court case. The judge granted my request. They assigned me my own confidential intermediary caseworker. I'll refer to her as Sarah, to keep her name confidential, just as their service implies.

Sarah called me on the phone to introduce herself to me shortly after I received the letter. She was a soft-spoken woman who shared with me that she had used the service to find her own daughter whom she had given up for adoption many years ago. She confided in me how much the reunion meant to the both of them and that this search was the best thing she had ever done. Sharing her intimate story with me helped me feel that Sarah was less of a stranger and put me more at ease. It also instilled hope in me for my own search. Sarah told me that because she was court-appointed, my records would now be open to her. She said she would keep me updated on her progress every couple of months by mail.

The next letter that came was not from Sarah, but from the courts, saying that all searches pending at this time with my agency would be halted—not just my case, but all searches. There was some litigation that had to be resolved before any court-appointed searches could continue. The letter also stated that every effort would be made to resolve this situation in a timely manner, that I would be kept informed on their progress through the mail, and that they were very sorry for the delay, but it could not be avoided.

I remember being very upset by this news and wondering how long the delay was going to take. After all, I had just begun my search and already there was a glitch. Still, I would try to remain optimistic and hope that everything would be resolved quickly. I took a big sigh of relief about six weeks later when I received a letter saying that the issue had been resolved and that all pending cases were to move forward again. I was grateful it hadn't taken too long.

Chapter 4

Back Burner

But my thoughts about my search would be diverted yet again.

Our son Joe confided to his father and me that he was having serious health issues that weren't going away. Joe was twenty-five years old at the time and was a heavy equipment operator by trade. He told us he was experiencing severe headaches and dizziness during the day at work. It would take all of his concentration just to take his next step when the symptoms would occur. After several visits with our family doctor provided no prognosis, and frustrated with no answers, the doctor finally ordered an MRI of Joe's brain. The answer came back in the form of a rare genetic disorder called *Chiari Malformation 1*.

Chiari Malformation is a structural defect in the cerebellum, the part of the brain that controls balance. Normally the cerebellum and parts of the brain stem sit in an indented space at the lower rear of the skull, above the foramen magnum (a funnel-like opening to the spinal canal). When part of the cerebellum is located below the foramen magnum, it is called Chiari Malformation. We finally had an answer, but we were afraid because it dealt with Joe's brain.

Joe was referred to a local neurologist, who his father and I went with him to see. After the doctor performed many medical tests in his office, he referred us to a neurosurgeon in Chicago.

This doctor was the top neurosurgeon in his field, in fact he was the head of the neurology department at the University of Illinois. The doctor had performed many surgeries dealing with Joe's problem, and he was respected by his peers. This put our family at ease.

To make a long story short, Joe only had two options available to him: either elect to have the surgery, which would include drilling a hole into the back of his skull to make more room for his brain and relieve some of the pressure there, or do nothing. The doctor gave us time to think it through.

This was not something that could be decided overnight, and ultimately, it would have to be Joe's decision, of course. No matter how old your child is, you still hurt when they hurt. You are there for them and hope they make the right choices in life, especially with a critical decision like this one, which could literally be life or death.

Joe ultimately decided to have the surgery, because his symptoms were only getting worse, and he was no longer able to deal with them. Joe said, "Enough is enough; let's do it." Although his father and I were beside ourselves with worry, we knew in our hearts that he had made the right decision, as there was really no other option.

Within a month of Joe's decision to go ahead, his surgery date was set, scheduled for May 15, 2005. The wait leading up to the surgery had been difficult for our entire family and especially for Joe. I remember researching what the surgery would entail and what would be expected. The neurosurgeon had gone over the procedure with us, which seemed scary enough, but as I wanted to know everything I possibly could, the Internet was a valuable tool.

Meanwhile Sarah had written; the prospect of locating my mother was looking very promising. She told me she had sent her a registered letter telling her of my interest in finding her or at least having some kind of written correspondence. Although this news from Sarah should have been of great significance to me at the time, all of my thoughts and concentration were now with my son. This would have to be put on the back burner until we knew he would be okay.

The morning of May 15, 2005 came quickly, and my entire family went to the hospital with Joe. I remember not being able to sleep at all the night before, praying that God would be watching over my son. I was afraid. I can only imagine what Joe was feeling. That morning was an early one because we had to be in Chicago by six o'clock. Of course, it was chaotic before we left; one of our dogs even ran away, which he had never done before, and he picked the worst time to do it.

We managed to get Joe to the hospital right on time, although we had to do eighty miles an hour to get there. I was happy our whole family was there to support Joe; I knew that we would be though, because we have always been a close family and love each other deeply. We took turns going into pre-op because only two people were allowed in at a time. We all told Joe we loved him and would be seeing him soon. We tried to joke around with him and make light of the scary situation. I remember trying to hold back the tears, thinking to myself, *What if I never see him again?* It was possible something could go horribly wrong; this was his skull they would be drilling a hole into after all. I think we all said our share of prayers that day, especially when the surgery lasted longer than anyone, including the doctors, had anticipated.

Six of the longest hours in our lives were spent waiting for the surgeon to come out of the operating room to tell us that Joe was doing fine, and the surgery had been a success. We all felt a great weight come off our shoulders, thanks to the skilled neurosurgeon and God who guided his hand. The moment I saw Joe after the surgery, I could tell the terrible pain he was in, and I wished I could have switched places with him. My husband and I spent the first night sleeping on the couches in the hospital waiting room within a few yards of Joe's hospital room. The doctors told us the first couple of days after a surgery can be critical, and Joe needed to be carefully monitored for such things as infection. We weren't going anywhere; we would be there if needed.

The hospital offered us an apartment that families can use to stay near their loved ones during recovery. It was very reasonably priced and within a few blocks. It was ideal, and we were very grateful. The apartment was basic, with a bed, a small kitchen, a couch, and TV. We were at the hospital bright and early every morning to visit Joe. It was great we were so close. Joe was still in a lot of pain, which the doctors said was to be expected after this type of surgery; they were giving him morphine to cope. On any given day, there would be about twenty interns and doctors in and out of Joe's room, accompanied by their clipboards and forms that they would check off as they asked Joe questions on how he was doing. This was also a teaching college and medical students did their internships right at the hospital. The doctors told us Joe was making good progress and that he was right on track with his recovery.

After a five-day hospital stay, the doctors released Joe. We set up a room at our house where he stayed for a few weeks until he got back on his feet. The first week he was very fragile and not very steady. Eventually he was able to walk down the block with me at his side to support him. We were happy to have our son back. Thanks to God.

Chapter 5

Dear Catherine Letter

Now that the health scare with my son was over, I could focus on the search for my mother. I knew Sarah had sent her a letter right around the time of my son's surgery and a year had passed already; She was slow to respond, or worse yet, didn't want to.

Finally, in June of 2006, Sarah called me one morning to say she had indeed located my mother. I could tell by the tone of her voice that this wasn't the news I was hoping for. Sarah told me my mother was not happy that our agency had located her; in fact, she was very upset by it. My heart sank as she told me. Even though I thought I had been searching only for my family history and heritage, who was I kidding? I was hurt by this news.

Although she was upset, my mother did write a couple paragraphs to answer the basic questions that I had regarding history. Sarah asked if I wanted her to read that letter over the phone, and I said yes.

The letter said:

You have requested medical information and family background. I can only answer concerning my family. Your father was a student who I never saw after I discovered I was pregnant. The most common cause of death [in my family] has been heart attack or stroke. My family members, even back several generations, have lived until their mid 80s. On my father's side, his grandparents emigrated from Sweden and Denmark in the 1880s/90s. My mother's ancestors came from England and Ireland, some in the 1880s, and others in 1830s. When I gave you up for adoption, it was with the expectation that you would be placed in a loving family situation. I hope this was the case. I have requested of Sarah that this be the only communication.

I have asked her not to contact me again. I hope you understand, or
at least do not think too badly of me.

This was certainly black and white. There was no gray area here. Nowhere to read between the lines. She washed her hands of me and wanted no further contact. That was that: hope you had a good life, good-bye. The letter was typed, not even hand-written. How cold and unfeeling of her.

I felt great sadness, but also anger that she hadn't taken more time and put more thought into writing the letter. Even though I was an adult, it still hurt. I could not distance myself from feeling the pain, even though I had been good at hiding my feelings throughout my life. Her words cut me like a knife.

After I had a while to let it sink in, I tried to make sense out of what she wrote and to rationalize it. I decided there were only two ways to look at it. The first would be that she was coerced into my adoption by her parents and society, who made her feel so ashamed and guilty for being an unwed mother, and that adoption was the only solution at the time. She had spent her entire life trying to forget the child she had given up so long ago. Perhaps I was opening up an old wound that she had worked long and hard to forget.

The second theory I had was that she just wanted to have a better life, and I did not fit into that picture.

I have chosen to believe the first theory. I did not want to harbor bad feelings toward my mother—I simply could not. I do not resent the fact that she made that decision, but I do resent that I will never have answers to some of the many questions that I feel I have the right to know the answers to. Answers that people who weren't adopted just take for granted.

Because I was still longing for answers after the emotionless letter my mother wrote, I did some research into adoptions during the 1950s when my adoption was finalized.

I came to find out that during that period of time, if a young woman was expecting and not planning to marry the father, adoption was considered a good option. In most cases, it was not that the young woman did not want to keep her baby or not even that she couldn't afford to raise her child. The bottom line was that the child was illegitimate, and society frowned upon women with illegitimate children. These mothers were told that adoption was a good way for them to get a second chance in life and to remain an upstanding member of society—a good solution for all concerned. After all, this was a win-win situation, as the baby would be placed with a couple who for whatever reason could not conceive a child of their own and the young mother would get a second chance at her life. The child would be raised in a two-parent family, and everyone would be happy. Often, the young woman was sent to a maternity home hidden away from society during the pregnancy. She would be taught the fine art of relinquishing her baby and encouraged to forget her pregnancy even happened in the first place. She should have no problem putting everything out of her consciousness and getting on with her life without her child.

Years later, many mothers wrote that relinquishing their babies was agony and that the anguish they suffered throughout their lives was immeasurable. They never forgot the babies they carried inside of them. The mother-child bond is not easily severed.

Reading that helped me to understand the letter my mother had written in response to my search. I believe my mother to be one of those girls who were led to believe that they would be able to carry on with life without giving it a second thought. I think that my mother probably carried a lot of shame and guilt inside and hurt deeply. This helped me to put her into a new light. I now have compassion and empathy for my mother and wrote this poem about how I can only imagine she felt.

> *I had no voice;*
> *They gave me no choice.*
> *Told me it was a new start;*
> *Broke my heart.*
> *Filled me with their shame;*
> *I know I was to blame.*
> *They underestimated our bond;*
> *They had no magic wand*
> *Told me I would soon forget;*
> *I have not yet.*
> *Told me many lies;*
> *But they would never hear my cries.*

To add insult to injury, the agency sent me a letter that I would have to fill out—a form saying that I would cease my search for my mother and her maternal bloodline. I had to have it notarized. *How official*, I thought. It hurt me to do it, but I complied and sent the form in.

For whatever reason, my mother was running scared. I had opened up a can of worms, and she wanted it closed back up. I believe she never told members of her family about my existence, including her younger brother and sister. My mother has probably been carrying this secret her whole life and may carry it to her death. Some days I feel optimistic—that one day she will have a change of heart and want to meet. I can think of nothing that would heal both of our old wounds better.

Until then, I respect her wishes and will leave her alone.

Chapter 6

Wounded

During this time, I had picked up a book that piqued my curiosity called *The Primal Wound*.

There have been numerous studies done on the effects of separation of a baby from its birthmother so soon after birth. Even though I certainly wasn't a child anymore, I was still grieving after reading my mother's letter. The author of *The Primal Wound* is Dr. Nancy Verrier, M.A. Not only did she write an influential book on these studies, but she offered the additional insight of being an adoptive mother herself.

Being a clinical psychologist and adoptive parent herself, Dr. Verrier believes that

> In working with adoptees, it is apparent that no matter what happens a month, a year, or several years in the future, that period immediately after birth...is a crucial period...At that time the mother is the whole world for the baby and his connection to her is essential....

> ...It is my belief, therefore, that the severing of that connection between the adopted child and his birthmother causes a primal or narcissistic wound, which affects the adoptee's sense of Self and often manifests in a sense of loss, basic mistrust, anxiety and depression, emotional and/or behavioral problems, and difficulties n relationships with significant others. (The Primal Wound, 21).

As Dr. Verrier also writes, "I was to discover during my ten years of research that...testing-out behavior was one of two diametrically opposed responses to having been abandoned, the other being a tendency toward acquiescence, compliance, and withdrawal. (ibid, xiii)"

The more that I read, the more the words that she said struck a deep chord within me. Ignorance is bliss, but the things I felt inside I could not deny. It was as if the words I was reading were jumping off the pages at me. I was the textbook child to a fault. I was compliant and never acted out. I would mostly numb myself to emotions, especially anger. I have little memory of expressing anger in childhood. I know I felt anger inside but didn't know of an outlet to release it, so I simply suppressed it. These articles stated that children who are truly secure in their life can express a range of emotions without thinking twice about it. I read in *The Primal Wound* that many of these children who suppressed their emotions, especially anger, suffered from gastro-intestinal problems as children. I had colic as a child and can remember the physical pain from having this condition. Dr. Verrier also stressed in her book the differences between the words *attachment* and *bonding*. These are two terms that are often used interchangeably.

Dr. Verrier states that

I believe that it would be safe to say that most adopted children form attachments to their adoptive mothers. This is a kind of emotional dependence, which may seem crucial to their survival. Bonding, on the other hand, may not be so easily achieved. It implies a profound connection, which is experienced at all levels of human awareness. (The Primal Wound, 19).

I know I established a connection with my mother. I am sure of that, but I am not sure if it would have been called bonding. I don't know for sure because I don't have any basis for comparison. This was the hardest thing for me to admit, because I know she would have wanted me to say we had bonded. She would always tell me how independent I had been as a child, perhaps this was one way to say I was distant with her at times. Another point that hit home with me was that many adoptees find it difficult to take any kind of criticism or ask others for help. This is something I have struggled with all my life. But it is only when we are confronted with our flaws, and recognize them in ourselves, that we can start to change.

Chapter 7

Seek and Ye Shall Find

Within a short time after sending the notarized letter saying that I would not continue to seek out my biological mother and her maternal family, I received another phone call from Sarah. She asked me if I wanted to do a separate search for my father.

Sarah told me there really wasn't much in my adoption files about him to go on, but that they could certainly try. My inclination at this point was to say, "Hell no," but maybe I'm a glutton for punishment, because for whatever reason I said yes.

Sarah said I would be assigned a new intermediary person to do this search. I was sad to see her go, because although we never actually met in person, I had talked to her many times and felt somewhat close to her because of our similar situations.

I was assigned a new intermediary person, whom I will call Mary, the name Catholic Charities gave to my biological mother in the letter they sent me so many years ago. A new search now began for my father. however my heart was not in it nearly as much this time, probably to distance myself from further hurt.

It had been a little less than a year since receiving my mother's letter when one day my phone rang. I was watching TV and the name of the agency came up through Caller ID on the TV screen. I ran to the phone to get the call, not knowing what to expect. I held out little hope of a positive outcome because the agency told me they really didn't have to much go on in my birth file.

Mary's voice was on the other end, and she sounded very happy. This time I sat at the kitchen table and braced myself for good news.

Mary said that she had indeed located my father and that he sounded thrilled by the news that I was trying to locate him. She said he sounded like a nice man, and he was very excited about the prospect of talking to me. My heart was racing with this news, and in fact, I was overwhelmed. I couldn't help being emotional, even though I kept telling myself I was only seeking medical and heritage information.

I had a hundred questions going through my head, but I simply asked Mary what the next step would be. She told me both my father and I would be receiving release forms in the mail, which we would both sign and mail back to the agency. As soon as they received both letters back, they would release the information to us at the same time. They would be sending us identifying information such as names, addresses, and phone numbers.

Who was I kidding? I was ecstatic about this outcome. I had reverted back to my childhood on Christmas morning, and the anticipation of opening presents under the tree. As corny as it sounds, that was exactly how I felt.

The next few mornings I waited for the mailman, because he usually delivered to our area before I left for work each day. When I received an envelope addressed to me with the agency's return address, I knew what I had been anticipating had finally arrived.

You would think I would have torn it open right away, but instead I stared at it for a while. My daughter Chrystal was home and told me if I didn't open it right then, she certainly would for me, as she was also excited. When I finally opened it, it actually had my father's name, address, and phone number— all as plain as day, right in front of me. You would have thought I won the lottery that day. I was filled with emotion that I had no control over. I was overwhelmed. I cried, and my daughter gave me a hug and told me she was proud of the fact that I hadn't given up. I can remember going into work that day and being almost in a trance. All I had on my mind was the thought of calling my father on the phone that night. I had told the ladies at work that I had received the letter, and they were all thrilled for me. I was so excited about contacting my father that day that I thought I would jump out of my skin. All I could think about was what I would say to him, and how I should approach the conversation. I had a hundred different questions I longed for answers to. But I didn't want to bombard him all at once and scare him off. What if, after I called him, he didn't like what I had to say and thought maybe this wasn't such a good idea anymore? I had come too far and

known each other for years—how ironic. There was no uneasiness when talking, as if we already had a connection somehow, someway.

I told him during our conversation that I did not want to intrude in his life, and after a slight pause, his voice cracked and then he openly broke down and cried. He told me that this was one of the best things that had ever happened to him.

He said, "In fact, this sort of thing just doesn't happen to people like me." He went on to say that he was truly excited.

In our first conversation, he told me my mother's name and how they had met. He said that they actually dated for a while in their senior year of high school. My father confided that he was never really 100 percent sure of my existence, since when my mother told him of her pregnancy, she told him never to contact her again. She had said that her family would help her to decide what to do. He told me he had felt vulnerable and that he felt like a child at the time even though he was nineteen.

He said that as a child he didn't have a stable upbringing, that he wasn't raised by his parents but was passed around a lot between relatives.

I told him I had no bad feelings toward him and that I understood his and my mother's situation.

All I really wanted from him now was to talk to him, to find out a little history, and maybe one day to actually meet. I wanted to look at him, look into his eyes, and hopefully find some similarities.

On the phone, my father had paused briefly before saying that he needed to tell me something important. I felt my heart drop as he told me he was confined to a wheelchair and that he had lost both of his legs due to diabetes about six years earlier. I told him I was sad to hear that news, and I hoped he and his family were dealing with it okay. He actually sounded relieved to get that off his chest, maybe he thought I would feel differently about him. How could anyone feel anything but sympathy after hearing that? My father told me that losing his legs had never slowed him down, that he was still a very active person in all respects. He said he had prosthetic legs that were specially fitted for him, and that he even had different shoes he could put on his feet either dress or casual. He also had a motorized golf cart, which he got around town in. He almost tried to make light of the situation, but I'm sure he must have had a difficult adjustment to make in every respect. I think a bit of my father's true character was showing through to me already.

My father went on to share with me that he had been married and divorced twice before his present marriage, but his current marriage had lasted twenty-five years, in fact his twenty-fifth wedding anniversary would be next month. He told me his wife's name was Donna and that she was only a year older than me. I have to admit I was a little blown away by the age difference but I thought to myself, *Good for him*. My father's age at the time we first spoke was sixty-eight and I was forty-nine.

We continued talking, and my father told me that he and Donna had a daughter together and her name was Darci; she was twenty-four. I thought to myself, *I have a sister less than half my age!*

He also shared with me he had three more children from his previous two marriages—two sons and a daughter. He told me he was the father of five children, including me. He told me I was his oldest and firstborn.

What a first conversation, I thought to myself. Not only am I talking to my biological father for the first time ever, but I find out that I also have four half-brothers and half-sisters. This was a lot for me to take in all at once, but even though I was overwhelmed, I was also very excited by the news.

Before we ended our first conversation, my father told me that he loved me. I was pretty blown away by this, but he sounded so sincere. He told me he would call me again very soon, and said he had my information too from the agency that located him.

He told me that this was the beginning of our new relationship as father and daughter.

I could not have been more thrilled. So much for just wanting family history and heritage!

Chapter 8

❖

Do You Know Who This Is?

After our first conversation, my father kept his word and called me shortly afterward.

When I answered the phone, he asked me if I knew who he was, that it was my father calling. It was always such a positive talk every time we spoke, almost as if we were both trying to make up for all the lost years that had passed. I sent him his first Father's Day card just a month after we spoke for the first time. Talk about trying to find just the right card—try to pick out a card for this situation. Even Hallmark doesn't make cards that read "Happy Father's Day from your daughter who you have just met after fifty years."

He sent me my first birthday card in June, which I'm sure must have been as equally difficult for him to find. Sometimes I felt like my father and I were two lost souls who, once we finally found each other, wanted everything to be perfect in every way and would not do anything to screw that up. I felt we were both childlike in that regard—it was very pure and innocent, like when you're a child meeting your first good friend and not knowing exactly what to say or do but knowing it is a good and positive life-changing experience for both of you.

The first birthday present my father sent me was a three-disc Celtic CD. I think he knew it would touch my heart and it did. During one of our many phone conversations over the summer, my father brought up my younger brother Jack's name, who still lived in the same hometown my father had been from. I asked him for my brother's phone number so that I could get in touch with him. My father thought this was a great idea and gave me his number.

I called him and left a message, "This is your sister Pat calling. I would love to talk to you, so if you get a chance, please call me back."

I think not five minutes passed and he called.

He simply said, "Hey, this is your brother Jack."

He said he really wasn't sure what to say to me, that this was new ground for him.

I replied, "Don't worry. I feel the same way that you do, believe me."

Jack told me on the phone that day that my father was very excited that I had contacted him, and he felt like this was truly a miracle that had happened.

Jack said he wanted to meet me; after all, we were related, we were brother and sister. We planned to get together for a barbeque at my house within the next couple of weeks. I was nervous and excited all at the same time. I had just recently contacted my father for the first time, and now I was making plans to meet my half-brother! I made sure my family would be home that day so they could meet their Uncle Jack. It's kind of ironic that while growing up, I had an Uncle Jack too.

The morning of the visit, Jack called to ask if it was all right if he brought his girlfriend Tammy and her little girl. At first I was afraid he was calling me to cancel our get-together. I was happy he was still coming, and I said I would love to meet his girlfriend. I even made a tray of fudge for him to take back home with him.

I was nervous in anticipation of his arrival, wondering what we would say to one another for our first meeting. I was sitting on my front stairs waiting impatiently for his arrival. A blue Ford pickup truck pulled into our driveway, and I knew it was him. I literally ran to open his car door, and when he got out, I gave him a big hug and kiss on the cheek. I could see the resemblance right off the bat. Jack had dark blond hair and hazel eyes, just like my son Joe. He had a longer torso and shorter legs, just like my kids and me. The shape of his face was the same. It's an amazing feeling, seeing someone who resembles you and knowing they are related to you.

He came into the house and sat our kitchen table with my family gathered around. At first I think he was a little nervous with all of us looking at him. I remember his right leg shaking and thinking, *My God, he even has the same mannerisms—I do that when I'm nervous. I do that too.*

Jack had brought pictures of him as a child, and our father Jerry was standing next to him. He also brought a picture of my father when he was eight or nine years old. It was like looking at a picture of my son at that age; it was surreal.

In fact, the next day I found one of my son's school pictures and put it next to my father's picture for comparison. The resemblance was amazing.

Jack shared stories with us of his time as a child. When our father came home from work after a long day and everything wasn't cleaned up and in its place, there would be hell to pay.

Father would be angry and make him straighten up right away. It sounded like our father had ruled with an iron fist. It also sounded like he had been a perfectionist. I hadn't met him yet, but I was hoping to soon, and I guessed I would find out for myself. Jack shared that he didn't get to spend much time with him as a child, since our father left early in the morning and came home late at night. To me, it sounded like there were hurt feelings between the two of them in their earlier years. I'm not sure this was true, it was just the feeling I got from Jack; maybe I was wrong, I hoped so. I could tell Jack cared about his father very much. That made me feel good.

Jack's profession at the time was a roofer, but I had gotten the impression that he was a jack-of-all-trades, no pun intended! Because Jack was in his forties, I'm sure roofing must have been physically challenging for him. I got the perception that he was a bit of a perfectionist, just like his father, and took pride in doing a good job. My son Joe is the same way—maybe it's in their blood.

Jack and I told each other that we would keep in touch. Although we haven't gotten together since that day, every once in awhile Jack will call me just to say hi and ask what's new. I am glad that I had the opportunity to meet him.

In one of my conversations with my father during the course of the summer, he told me of a devastating story of how one of his younger brothers was hit and killed by a car when crossing a busy street on his way home from school. His other brother had been walking with him and had witnessed the accident, and he had never been able to forgive himself for not being able to save him.

After the tragedy, his older brother enlisted in Vietnam, not caring much about his own life anymore. The guilt, even though not justified, would consume him. I thought to myself how very sad it was that he would blame himself for something out of his control, an accident. In reality, there was probably little that he could have done. While he was in Vietnam, the brother and a few of the troops were captured by Vietcong and imprisoned in very harsh conditions. His brother would go on to save one of his fellow soldier's lives. He would literally carry him to safety. In the process of doing this, he had every knuckle on both hands broken. In a way, maybe this helped fill the hole he had in his heart after his brother had died. This is the story of a true hero, and he was given a prestigious medal for his act of courage.

Chapter 9

Off to Delaware

It was sometime in the month of July that I told my father I really wanted to meet him in person. Bob and I had a week off for vacation in September, and I could think of no better way we could spend our time than to meet him. He agreed wholeheartedly, and our trip was set. The ladies at my work even started a collection to help with my trip. I was touched by this. They were truly excited for me.

The drive to Delaware to meet my father seemed so surreal. I'm sure anticipating my arrival was surreal to him as well. How could it not be? I thought of buying him a gift, but decided to write him a poem instead. I labored over what I wanted to say, but in the end I felt I had found the words to tell him how I truly felt.

Right before we were scheduled to leave, his wife Donna told me on the phone that he wasn't doing so well physically due to a heart condition he had. This was the first time I heard about his heart. Donna said that we better hurry up and get there. I asked her if she was sure that we should come, and she told me he would be very upset if we didn't. He had been looking forward to our meeting, and I might not get another chance. I didn't tell her, but I would have been devastated if we didn't go. Looking back, she was probably guided by intuition. While I was packing my bags, I asked God to please let him hold on. *God, you have always come through before; please don't stop now.*

We decided to drive there and stop halfway to spend the night. We were driving from Illinois to Delaware and made Ohio our stopping point. Ironically, this was the birth state of my father, although we didn't know at the time.

We picked a great time to travel because it was fall, and the leaves on the trees were at their most brilliant color with reds and golds and deep purples. We drove through the mountains on our way there, which was breathtaking. It helped to distract my thoughts of how nervous I was about meeting my father for the first time.

I read that it is healthy to want to know your roots, where you began, whose blood flows through your veins. My mind was racing in anticipation of how I would feel when I first laid eyes on him—it was overwhelming to me. I pictured that I would see him from a distance, know right away that it was him, and run up to him, throwing my arms around his neck and saying something funny like, "Hey, where have you been all my life?"

We pulled up to his home and into his driveway, which was by far the widest driveway I had ever seen. We would find out later that my dad worked with asphalt in his younger years, and he certainly had spared none here.

As we walked to his home, Donna came running out to meet us and yelled to my father who was still in the house, "She's your daughter all right!"

I wasn't quite sure what she had meant; maybe I resembled my brothers and sisters and she was just letting him know this in advance. Donna led us into the kitchen and there big as life, sitting in his wheelchair, was my father with a big smile on his face.

I was frozen inside with anticipation but managed to bend over and give him a hug and a kiss on the cheek. I could tell he was on the verge of crying. He had a kind face and beautiful blue eyes that were welling up with tears. It was surreal to me that I was standing in front of my father and looking into his eyes for the first time. I was suppressing my emotions and did not cry, but I was experiencing some pretty powerful feelings inside.

I thought we would sit down and talk, but the next thing you know we were being whisked off to dinner at one of their favorite local diners. It felt like Bob and I were in a whirlwind. We were all a little nervous at first, not knowing what to expect from one another and not knowing what to say. We were just making small talk, but what did I expect—him to tell his whole life story at dinner? I loved his voice; you could tell he was from Chicago by his accent.

After dinner, we headed back to his home, and he took us on a tour of his house. They had a beautiful ranch style home, and the décor was very nice. I noticed right away that he had a lot of American Indian artwork on display in a tall glass cabinet in the living room. His collection was of Indian sculpture and included many beautiful works. He told me he loved learning about their history and culture. We had this in common; I also loved learning about Indian history. He also was a collector of amazing clocks from around the world. They each had a different chime and would sound at different hours throughout the day.

During the tour of their home, my father led us into a room he said we would be sleeping in, which turned out to be my sister Darci's room. They had kept it exactly the same way that she had it when she lived there. It was decorated with many of her cheerleading pictures along with a collection of trophies she had won. Darci shared with us later that her mother and father were her biggest fans, never missing one of her competitions. Darci had moved out and now shared a place with Sean who we would eventually meet.

On the headboard of the bed was a wooden plaque, which simply read "Believe." My father told me he purchased this for me, and it was mine to keep. This certainly touched my heart.

Donna had to work the next day, so she had to turn in early. My father had been retired from his job for some time now. Bob, my father, and I sat in the living room as he told us the history of Delaware. Donna's family was from there, and they liked it so much that he decided to retire there. He seemed proud of the history of the state—that it was the first state in the union.

He told us that he had worked for the same family for over twenty-five years, driving a truck for his living straight out of high school. He felt he was more like a family member than a worker after knowing the family for so long. You could tell he was very proud of his work. He also laid asphalt, and he made no reservations that he was good at what he did—that he was a perfectionist. The trucking company was where he met Donna; they fell in love and married. A few years later, Darci was born. They lived in a suburb of Chicago for many years, until they moved to Delaware after his retirement. When he first retired, my father had a big adjustment to make, going from the hustle and bustle of Chicago to the peacefulness and serenity of Delaware.

It was very quiet here and reminded me of country living—just what the doctor ordered. Bob was tired from doing all of the driving that day and said good night. This just left my father and me. I had asked him if we could stay up, just the two of us, and he said of course. I actually wasn't tired at all, and I think I was running on pure adrenaline.

My father sat in his favorite recliner chair, positioned in front of the TV. He had a white sheet covering the lower half of his body like a blanket. I sat within a few feet of him on the couch to his left. When I looked in his direction, I could see his full profile, and he turned in my direction when he spoke to me. The TV was on, but the volume was turned low so we could hear each other when we spoke. I started out the conversation by asking him about his childhood, and if it was a happy one.

He replied after a slight hesitation, "Not really." He added that he was passed around from aunt to aunt, that he had no stability in his younger years.

I thought that it shed some light on why his marriages didn't last. At least he found stability with his current wife Donna, because they had been married for twenty-five years now.

I remember thinking to myself that night that I was starting to get to know my father, and what a miracle it truly was. I didn't waste too much time before I asked him the question I had wondered about for a very long time—how he and my mother met and how I came about.

I began by explaining that I had also done a search for my mother, but that she had said that she wanted no further contact with me in no uncertain terms. He turned in my direction and looked very shocked by this. He told me he couldn't believe it; that she had always been an A+ in his book. He truly seemed baffled that she hadn't wanted any communication with me.

He said they had met in high school and that they had dated for long time, over a year. He said they were from the same neighborhood. He told me he had gotten to know her entire family quite well. He looked at me and told me my mother's name. He also told me her younger sister and brother's names—my aunt and uncle—who I believe didn't even know of my existence. Her mother's name was Catherine, and he said she had an Irish accent that he loved to hear. My mother's father was a postmaster for a large district, and he had gotten my father a job when he was in high school. He said he had worked at the post office for a short time for her father.

When my mother shared with my father that she was pregnant, she said she never could see him again. She said she would figure out what to do with the help of her parents, that it was no longer his worry or concern. My father said he had felt helpless and powerless. At the time he was nineteen years old and my mother was eighteen. I'm sure that society and my mother's parents, along with the Catholic Church, made her decision for her. She must have felt very vulnerable, with her back up against the wall so to speak. Maybe my father was happy to be let off the hook, but I also think he had regrets and probably thought about me from time to time throughout his life. He had told me on the phone the first time I spoke to him that he wasn't 100 percent sure of my existence, but I think he might have told me that due to guilt he must have had dealt with for a very long time.

Perhaps he thought I would think badly of him or even be ashamed of him for not trying to find me or locate me throughout the years. But in reality, this could not have been further from the truth. I have never judged him, nor will I ever judge him. I think he was a young and vulnerable man. At that time, a young unmarried couple had no resources available to them. Society and the church dictated the appropriate thing to do, and parents would not be any help either, after all, this would save their reputations too. What a neat little package with all of the loose ends tied up. How could they be so blind?

I believe my mother must have suffered very deeply from the separation of mother and baby. How could she not? I'm sure at the time that both she and my father felt the weight of the world on their shoulders with no direction to turn. I do not hold any grudges against my mother or father. At that time, how could a young couple contend with two superpowers like society and the church?

I asked my father the million-dollar question that night, and that was if he loved my mother. This time he did not hesitate with his answer; it was yes.

Waking up the next morning in my father's home was still surreal to me. Bob and I walked into the kitchen where my father was already sitting in his wheelchair looking out the window.

I couldn't help but wonder if he had been thinking about our conversation the night before; if it had impacted him as much as it did me, and if he was thinking what a miracle it was for the both of us. Standing in front of his wheelchair that morning, I was consumed with emotion and felt my eyes well up with tears. I told him how much our conversation had meant to me. I apologized for keeping him up so late the night before. He told me he hadn't minded at all, that our talk meant the world to him too.

My father said he was anxious to show us his property outside, since we hadn't had much time the day before. He led the way in his wheelchair, which he maneuvered pretty well. We walked alongside him as he took us for a tour of the backyard. His neighbor was working in her yard, and he yelled out a greeting to her.

She responded, "Hey, Jerry, how you doing?"

My father struck me as a very friendly, outgoing guy. When I was a young child growing up, I was extremely shy and would usually hide in my room when my mother had relatives stop by our house. It would take a lot of coaxing to get me to even come out. I wondered if my father had also been painfully shy as a young boy. There were so many questions I hoped for answers to. I thought I would have all the time in the world to spend with him.

He continued to show us his beautifully landscaped backyard, which had many different flowers and bushes all varying in color and size. He told us that he and Donna had done all the work themselves. Even though he was disabled, it hadn't stopped him from doing what he loved. Whimsical statues were set up in random places, and in the center of the yard was a huge lighthouse about ten feet tall. It had a light on top just like a beacon on a real lighthouse. The light illuminated the yard at night; it was beautiful. It was obvious they had both done a lot of hard work and it really paid off. I'm sure they must have been proud of their accomplishments.

We went around to the front yard, which had also been meticulously landscaped. There was a pond in front of the house that had running water. It sounded very peaceful as the water hit the stones my father had placed within the fountain. He told Bob and me that he had done all the work himself, sitting on the ground and actually digging out the earth with a hand tool. It must have taken him many hours; I don't know if I could have had the determination that he did.

It proved once again that my father's disability did not deter him from what he set his mind to accomplish. I really respected him for that.

I asked my father and Bob to wait outside while I ran into the house to grab my camera, which I had made sure to bring along. I began to take pictures of him and Bob and his beautiful home and the surroundings. Then I handed the camera to Bob and asked him to take a picture of my father and me. I'm so grateful that picture was taken because, as it would turn out, it is the only picture we have together. Later when I returned home, I put it into a frame that read, "With God all things are possible." I knew I would treasure it forever.

While we were still outside, I walked over to our jeep, which was parked in the driveway, and opened the car door to get out the poem I had written for my father. I had framed it myself. I was sitting within arm's reach of his wheelchair as I read him my poem. About halfway through, I started to get emotional because it was so unreal to me to be standing next to my father and reading my heartfelt thoughts to him.

When I finished reading, he looked up at me and with true sincerity told me thank-you. He said no one had ever written a poem for him, and he was truly touched. I guess my father and I were both cut from the same cloth, both emotional people. He admitted openly to me that he was very emotional and would cry watching movies or books sometimes. He wasn't the least bit ashamed by these emotions; I liked that about him. Not many men can admit they have these feelings without grimacing a bit.

We saw a man walking up to the driveway, and with a huge smile on his face my father said, "Here comes my best friend Sal."

My father introduced Bob and me, saying to Sal, "I would like you to meet my daughter Patricia from Illinois."

It was obvious that his best friend had heard a lot about me leading up to my visit. Sal gave me a big hug and said how anticipated my visit had been; it made me feel good. I may have even spotted a tear in Sal's eye.

We went to breakfast that morning at the local International House of Pancakes. During breakfast, my father told us it took him about two or three years to adjust to life in Delaware after the hustle and bustle of living and working in Chicago. He and Bob got along quite famously as they had similar backgrounds, both being raised in Chicago.

My father told us that when he was a young boy he had received a slingshot for a present one year. He took aim and killed a baby bird in a tree. How he felt so bad about it—that it was a baby and all—that he took the little bird and buried it. He never took out his slingshot again.

After breakfast, we decided to go to Rehoboth Beach, which was located about ten minutes from my father's home. It was extremely hot that day, probably in the upper eighties, but also uncomfortable because of the humidity. When we arrived there, it was peaceful with the ocean waves hitting the beach. There were many little quaint shops and restaurants running up and down the boardwalk. My father was in his wheelchair. I pushed him up to the sand by the water, and we watched the waves come in together as father and daughter. It is a moment frozen in time in my memory.

This time we had together would leave many imprints in my mind; maybe because it was so profound to me. It was almost as if somewhere in my subconscious I was being told, *You might not have too many of these memories together, so you better store them in a safe place.*

Because it was so hot, we didn't stay very long; I could tell this outing was draining my father of energy, so we drove back to his home. We relaxed for a while until Donna came home from work. When she arrived, I could tell she was upset with him for not calling her during the day and letting her know how he was feeling. He probably called her regularly during the day, and I don't blame her for being concerned, especially because of his health problems.

That night, my father and Donna invited their best friend Sal and his wife to join us for dinner. I could tell how fond Donna and my father were of their friends and how they truly enjoyed each other's company.

There was a lot of laughter and good conversation that night—everyone was having a good time. Sal told a story of one day when my father and the neighbor lady, who was also disabled, decided to take a car ride together. They ended up getting into an accident, and my father's prosthetic legs ended up in the middle of the street. The EMT arrived at the scene and phoned into his dispatch that this accident probably involved a fatality because the poor guy's legs were scattered about the street. The EMT was quite relieved when he found out they were only fake legs. Everyone had a good heartfelt laugh that night remembering the incident. I had a feeling there were probably a lot more funny stories like that one, because my father and his friends were quite the characters, and they all had a great sense of humor. Even though they were older, they were still young at heart, this was obvious.

After dinner that night, we all sat outside on the screened-in porch attached to the huge pole barn Darci's boyfriend had helped build. Sitting in his chair, my father told me that his mother—my grandmother—had had a good heart, and he wished he could have spent more time with her growing up. He never elaborated on why he didn't, and I never asked him that night. I thought that there would always be an opportunity to ask later. After all, we had all the time in the world, didn't we? He also told me that my grandmother's ancestors were from England. I thought, what a match: my mother an Irish Catholic and my father an English Protestant. My mother's family probably had a few reservations at the start of their relationship, I'm sure.

My sister Darci and Sean also came to visit that night. Bob and I were standing outside as they pulled up in their car. Darci was a beautiful young woman with a petite build and fragile features. She had blonde hair and blue eyes, with a pretty smile to match. We gave each other hugs and said hello. I wondered what she thought of this situation. I'm sure she must have had a million questions about me, and I'm sure she must have had some reservations too. After all, I pretty much came out of nowhere to meet my father, who was her father too. Maybe she felt a little protective of him. I wouldn't blame her for having those feelings—I'm sure I would under the circumstances—but if she did, she never let on.

Darci appeared to be quiet and reserved, and she reminded me of myself when I was her age. Sean was a nice looking young man, who came up and introduced himself to us and shook Bob's hand. We found out Sean was an electrician and had his own business; he struck me as a pretty sharp guy. There was an obvious respect shown for Darci, and you could tell he genuinely cared deeply for her. It was refreshing to see a young couple so much in love; it just made you feel good. It was exciting for me to meet my sister—my own flesh and blood. It's a feeling I can't explain, but it felt right to me.

Later that evening, my father said that all of a sudden he wasn't feeling well, something was wrong. Donna, who of course had gone through countless of episodes with him, seemed concerned. I found out they had been in and out of the hospital many times throughout their life together; they were no strangers to this. My father was being stubborn and didn't want to go in, saying they would more than likely keep him in the hospital for awhile and that we were here on vacation. We told him his health was our only concern; we didn't think twice. With a lot of coaxing from his wife and daughter Darci, he relented and went in.

We followed Donna and Darci to the hospital in our car. On the way there, Bob and I just looked at each other in shock, not even knowing what to say. Was he going to die while we were here visiting? This couldn't be happening.

My father was not a well man, but he had put on a gallant effort for us. Everyone at the hospital knew him by name; he was a frequent flier there. The doctor said he was retaining a lot of water, especially in the stomach area. His stomach had the appearance of being swollen up, just like a balloon. They hooked him up to IVs and gave him a diuretic to help him pass the water he was retaining. In the hospital that evening, I found out that my father also had a pacemaker in his chest that would keep his heart beating if it ever stopped. I thought, this man has no legs and a weak heart, but such a strong spirit. I remember calling my daughter Chrystal and explaining what was happening with him in the hospital. She was studying to become a nurse, and she said it sounded like congenital heart failure with him retaining so much water. At that point, my father was admitted into the hospital and stayed there for the rest of our visit. Bob and I decided we would stay with him and prayed he would recover.

The next couple of days were like a roller-coaster ride for Bob and me. We didn't know what to expect.

So many thoughts were consuming my mind. Was he going to live? Or would he die while we were there? Was my visit too much for him to take? Donna had reassured us that he had been a sick man for a long time now and that it was not related to our visit. Once again, I prayed that he would pull through this.

My father told us he had had so many plans for us during our visit and being in the hospital wasn't on the top of his list. I remember him mentioning on one of many of our phone conversations during the summer that he wanted to take us on a ferryboat ride from Delaware to New Jersey. He also said he had wanted to show us Washington DC. I know he was very interested in the history of these areas and also was proud of it, which was obvious when he spoke. He had been so excited about meeting us and showing us around. I'm sure he was very disappointed that this would not be happening, not on this trip anyway. I told him not to give it a second thought, that we had all of the time in the world. After all, he would get well, and we would be back soon for another visit.

One thing that was apparent—my father was not a complainer. I'm sure that he must have been in a lot of pain, but he never let it show or said anything about it. He had a strong character. He told us about his hospital stay seven years earlier in Washington. This was where he had both legs amputated from the knees down. He said that after the operation he was given morphine to help him cope with the intense pain, and it had given him horrible nightmares. He mentioned one specific nightmare where he was on a roller coaster, and it was dark out, and he couldn't see where he was going. He said it was terrifying.

Although this was certainly not the ideal situation, we were still grateful for spending time with him. I'm sure this must have been very difficult for Donna. After all, she knew she could very well be losing her husband and partner of twenty-five years, and I know she must have hurt deeply. She was very accommodating to us under these stressful circumstances. In fact, with my father's urging, she took us back to Rehoboth Beach the next day. He thought it would be good for everyone to get away from the hospital for a while.

It turned out to be a very nice day, which we spent walking along the boardwalk and going into some of the little shops there. We also walked along the beach and watched as the waves came into shore. Just a couple days earlier, my father was with us doing the same thing. I missed him not being there with us this time.

I felt a little guilty that he was sitting in the hospital room while we were at the beach.

Feelings can change so quickly. In the beginning, all I was looking for was medical and heritage information, and now I was missing him. I already felt a connection between us. Maybe it happened so quickly because subconsciously we knew we wouldn't have much more time together here on earth. Even though things were not picture perfect, I will never regret having met him—it was life changing for me, and I hope and for him too.

We walked back to my father's hospital room that afternoon. We sat and talked about what we did at the beach that day, and he seemed happy that we had gone and not sat there and been cooped up all day.

While we were there, the hospital chaplain peeked into the room and asked if my father wanted to talk to him and said he would be available if my father needed him. Right away, I associated the presence of the priest with the last rites, which is a sacrament given by the Catholic Church before you die. I felt very uneasy and emotional, remembering when the priest came to visit my mother at our home.

Our parish priest had made many visits to my mother since she could not leave the house because she was so sick. He would bring her communion, talk to her for a while, and say the rosary with her.

When the priest was in my father's room that afternoon, I felt like standing up and yelling, "My father's not ready for last rites. He's not even close to that!"

But I also felt like saying to him, "Please stay. I need someone to talk to, because I feel lost inside." I never said a word though, keeping silent once again. After the priest left, we all started to talk again.

I felt myself staring at my father's face as he spoke. It was as if I was trying to memorize every detail, as if somehow I knew I wouldn't get too many more chances for this. I wanted to remember his face. He had a kind face with beautiful blue eyes. He had my father's face.

During the conversation that afternoon, he stopped mid-sentence and turned in my direction. With his right index finger pointed directly at me, he said, "You know, you have your mother's eyes." With that, he had blown me away for the second time. The first was when he told me that he had loved me during our very first phone conversation. He had the power to do this—to knock me off my feet.

Our trip was coming to an end, and my father was still cooped up in the hospital room. It made Bob and me very uneasy to say good-bye to him like that. At the time, I didn't realize I would never see him again.

When I thought about my trip later, I realized there had been a lot of "firsts and lasts" that happened between us:

The first and last time we met.

The first and last time we saw each other's faces and looked into each other's eyes.

The first and last time we hugged.

The first and last heart-to-heart talk we had together in person.

I bought my father a red carnation and handed it to him that last day in the hospital. He told me he loved carnations and said they always made a suite coat look nice if worn in the lapel.

We spoke of our plans to get together in the future. He told us he couldn't wait to meet his grandchildren and great-grandchildren. I gave him a hug and told him I loved him and would see him soon. He hugged me back and said he loved me too.

I could have easily cried but held my emotions in and told him, "Let's not get emotional now," as we would surely see each other again.

Looking back at our last words in the hospital room that day, I wish I would have shown him more emotion, because I wouldn't be given that chance again. But somehow, I think he knew how I felt about him.

Before we left, we thanked Donna for her hospitality, especially during such a difficult time. Donna told us we were always welcome there; in fact, she hoped we could make their house our summer vacation home from time to time. We also said good-bye to Darci and Sean that day. I gave her a hug and told her how much it meant to me to meet her and my father. We told each other that we would keep in touch, and I'm happy to say that we really have.

Even with such loving good-byes, we left Delaware that day with heavy hearts.

Chapter 10

Not Ready for Good-byes

Within a week of coming back from Delaware, Donna was on the phone, telling us that my father was now under hospice care. A nurse would come to their home to check on my father and help him with whatever he needed, like medications and basic care. I had heard of hospice before but didn't really know a great deal about the organization. I didn't want to accept the fact my father was dying and naively thought that hospice was there to help him recuperate. When I told my best friend Carmen about this, she told me this was the end of the road for my father.

She told me this out of love, so I would be aware of what was happening and could start to accept it. Although ignorance is bliss, I really did need to fully understand.

I felt the need to do something for my father, so I made a blanket in a native Indian design and sent it to his home in Delaware. It was now October of 2007 and I thought it would be a good gift for the coming winter months. He called me to thank me for the blanket and told me how warm it was. He also said how much he enjoyed seeing me on our visit, but he never said again that he would be visiting us. I thought he knew that he didn't have much time left.

The next time I spoke to Donna, she told me she didn't think he would live to see his sixty-ninth birthday, which was the next month. My father called me on a Thursday evening in the middle of October to say that he loved me and asked me to tell Bob and the kids too. I promised him I would and told him I loved him too. He sounded so tired on the phone that night.

That next Saturday morning, my father took his last breath—in his home, with Donna nearby. Donna stopped his favorite antique clock at the time of his death. The chime no longer sounded at his home in Delaware.

Donna called our home and actually spoke to Bob when she told us of my father's passing. She said he had gone peacefully. Bob came to me with tears in his eyes to tell me. Even though you think you are prepared for such news, you never really are. You always hold out some kind of hope. I think I may have been in shock at first, because I didn't react with tears. I just felt numb.

Later, I did go through the range of emotions, including anger, sadness, despair, disbelief, and finally, acceptance that he was really gone. He had vanished from my life as quickly as he had come into it—we were two passing ships in the night. It took me a while to truly appreciate our meeting and what a blessing it had been.

Bob had told me that I had been robbed. After all, we had just started to get to know each other, and the next thing you know he was gone. At first I agreed with his way of thinking; after all I was devastated about the news. There was so much more I wanted and needed from the relationship. Somehow though, the more I thought about it, the more I realized there were two ways to look at it. Either I had been robbed, or our meeting had truly been a gift from God. I had met my father after fifty years, and then he passed away within a month of us meeting each other for the first time. What are the odds of that happening? The poem I wrote said never to doubt God's infinite wisdom. I have chosen to believe that God has a plan for us all, and everything in life happens for a reason. We should never doubt him. Therefore, I am grateful for what he has given me. I feel as if divine intervention was at play here, and it touched both of our lives.

There are two ways to look at life. Either every day is a miracle, or there are no miracles at all. Albert Einstein

Donna said she wanted to have a private service for my father at his home in Delaware. I told her we wouldn't miss it for the world; we would be there. Within a few weeks, Bob and I were back in our jeep headed to Delaware once again, this time with heavy hearts. Most of the ride was a blur this time. It was only a month earlier that I was filled with joy and anticipation before arriving at his home.

When my mother Margaretrose passed away in my early twenties, I can remember the empty feeling I had walking into my childhood home after her funeral. I was not looking forward to experiencing this emptiness again, but it was something I needed to do for closure. I have always believed in God and was certain in my heart that both my adoptive mother and my birth father were with him.

In one of our many phone conversations over the summer, my father told me he believed in God but didn't think he needed to attend church to prove it. He said he thought God had a special place in his heart for children who died. He believed that these children would sit on his lap in heaven. He said there was true beauty in the face of a child.

I remember my father telling me that he didn't think he was a nice person. All I could see was that he had a good heart. Who could make a comment like that if they didn't have a good heart? I know people tend to make saints out of many people who die. I realize that my father certainly had flaws, but he was human just like all of us. We are all imperfect. I know in my heart that he was a good man.

We had stopped at a roadside flower stand and picked out a beautiful white mum to give to Donna. We pulled up to my father's home in Delaware, almost expecting him to come out and greet us in his wheelchair. I felt an uneasy and lonely feeling inside, knowing this would not happen.

Now all that remained were his ashes that were placed in an urn on top of a table Donna had set up in the front yard. It was nicely arranged with my father's significant memorabilia, his empty wheelchair, and the poem that I had written him, which was on top of the table.

It made me feel good that Donna had included me in the family like that. It meant a lot to me. About fifty white chairs had been set up in rows on the lawn. The front chairs closest to the memorabilia table were reserved for the family, which had included Bob and me. We sat with Donna and Darci and her fiancé, Sean. There was also Donna's family: her mother and father, her brother, and her nieces. The people who were noticeably missing in my eyes were my father's other three children. Where were they? Why didn't they show up for their own father's service? *How sad*, I thought to myself. What could have kept them from attending? I didn't know the whole story and may never know it entirely. Maybe I'm better off not knowing.

It was a beautiful warm October day in Delaware, with the sun shining down on the group assembled in the front yard. The sky was a deep shade of blue. I specifically remember beams of white from the sun hitting the table, making various patterns of light. It was as if God himself was telling us he was present and accounted for. I have always felt that there are signs all around us; we just need to look for them.

Donna's father was a minister and said the opening prayers at a podium set up for the service. He then asked if anyone wanted to approach the podium to say a few words.

My father's best friend Sal stood right away and walked up with a written eulogy in hand. My father had been his best friend for many years; you could tell right away that Sal was shaken up. I liked Sal the first time I met him—you could tell he had a heart of gold. Although he tried his hardest, he could not get past his first sentence without crying. He tried two or three times, but just couldn't do it. It was very emotional to watch; you knew how much my father had truly meant to him.

Another good friend tried to say a few words and also got choked up. At this point, the friend's wife took over for him and said what good friends they had all been together throughout the years. How there had been so much joy and laughter in their lives, how my father would be sorely missed, but never forgotten.

My sister Darci got up and went to the podium next. She had written a letter to him and read it to us. She shared her heartfelt thoughts and feelings about her father; it was very emotional. You could tell she was devastated about losing him. I have spoken with her many times since, and she told me she thinks about him all the time. She has many good memories. She told me he is her guardian angel.

Donna's father walked up to the podium after Darci had finished and asked again if anyone else wanted to share anything. I stood up and said I wanted to say something. This was very uncharacteristic of me—in fact, I hated this kind of thing, and it made me nervous. But I thought to myself, *This is something that I need to do because I will never get this chance again. It is now or never.*

I started out by introducing myself, because I was sure most people there didn't know me.

I told everyone that the first time my father and I spoke to each other on the phone, that he put me at ease right away. It was if we had known each other for years. He had accepted me with open arms and heart. I told them how the very first time that we spoke he said loved me. And how that blew me away—not ever expecting such a show of emotion from someone who didn't even know me. I told them how much he had touched my life in so many ways, and how I would never forget him.

Donna was the last of my father's loved ones to talk. She spoke of his sense of humor and the many memories she would hold onto. I knew she would miss him deeply. I also know it must have been a tremendous strain on her throughout the years, especially being in and out of the hospital so many times. She was always by his side to help him, especially when he became disabled.

One of her nieces stood up and sang "Amazing Grace." She had a beautiful soprano voice, and the moment was very emotional.

There were probably seventy people who showed up to pay their respects. My father was well loved by so many. All in all, it was a very moving service—a tribute to my father's life and a clear indication of how he will be missed by so many.

After the service, the family all received red roses. Donna had put pictures in the yard on easels. The pictures were of my father at various ages throughout his life, mainly with Donna and Darci.

One of my father's best friends approached me after the service. He took my hand and placed it between his. He looked into my eyes and told me that he had promised my father that he would tell me how much my meeting him had meant to my father—that it had been one of the best things that ever happened to him. I really needed that reassurance; it meant the world to me to hear it. I was certainly happy that we made it to his service.

The service had been emotional, and Bob had shed some tears. He too had experienced a loss. In that short amount of time, he had gotten close to my father. It was sad that they could not have known each other longer.

My father's best friend Sal made a point of coming up to us after the service to tell us that my father had planned a trip with him to come to Illinois to visit us next spring, and that he had wanted to meet his grandchildren and great-grandchildren. I think that hit me the hardest emotionally, that he was actually planning a trip to see us. My family could have met their grandfather and great-grandfather. This would have meant the world to everyone. Now I could only tell them how special he was.

Darci found out she was expecting a child not long after our father's passing. I know she missed him greatly, and she said he would have made a wonderful grandfather to her child. She said that now he would be her and her baby's guardian angel and would watch over them. Darci gave birth to a beautiful baby girl in October—one year after our father's death. Even though Darci

Conclusion

I think that adoptees can have a picture-perfect upbringing with their adoptive parents, and yet still feel the need to find their roots; it's a natural, maybe even primal, need. Adoptive parents, if still alive, should not feel threatened by this desire. It is a testament that they have raised a well-rounded child. I encourage all adoptees to seek out their history as it is a part of who they are. They may find more than they had ever hoped for.

Many, if not most, adoptees search for their biological mothers first. This is understandable because of the maternal bond. In some cases, such as my own, this search leads to a dead end for one reason or another. In the beginning, when I was asked if I wanted to find my biological father, I was reluctant. This was because I was deeply hurt by my mother's decision to not allow contact with me, even though I tried to rationalize her thinking.

My decision to go ahead with the search for my father was one of the best decisions I have ever made. Even though it was short-lived, it was still a gift that was given to me.

For many different reasons, a father may not search for his baby that was relinquished in the past. He may had felt excluded from the adoption itself, as if he didn't have much say in what happened to his own flesh and blood. He may have been young and naïve, as my own father was. Whatever the reason, these fathers are human beings and can grieve the loss in their lives too. They may wonder about their child throughout their lives. I'm sure this isn't the case for all, but I bet it is for the majority. They may wish that one day their child will try to contact them. Fathers are half of the equation, and although they don't carry their child as a mother does for nine months, they are important and should not be forgotten.

Like an iceberg that is buried within the oceans depths; with only its tip visible above the surface of the water, so is the adoptee's history buried, waiting to be uncovered. Little by little, he will chip away at the layers, and with persistence and skilled tools he will be able to uncover his past, his beginning.

References

Fessler, Ann. *The Girls Who Went Away.* U.S.A.: The Penguin Press, a member of the Penguin Group(U.S.A.), 2006.

Verrier, Nancy Newton. *The Primal Wound : Understanding the Adopted Child.* Baltimore: Gateway Press, 1993.